Reminiscences...

George Saunders

A

REMINISCENCES

Geo. Saunders

REMINISCENCES

BY

GEORGE SAUNDERS, C.B., M.D.

DEP.-INSP.-GEN. OF HOSPITALS

London

JAMES NISBET & CO., LIMITED

22 BERNERS STREET, W.

1907

CLR

Printed by BALLANTYNE, HANSON & Co.
At the Ballantyne Press, Edinburgh

PREFATORY NOTE

IN publishing these Reminiscences I may mention that they are also appearing in a Japanese version by my friend, Count Uesugi, who has taken so kind an interest in my work both in the Far East and in England that he is bringing it to the notice of his countrymen, with a special Preface of his own.

G. S.

LONDON, *July* 1907.

CONTENTS

REMINISCENCES

EARLY LIFE

I WAS born at Cork on the 10th October 1823. My father, of whom I was the fourth son, was Lieut.-Colonel Richard Saunders, first of the 60th Rifles and afterwards of the Royal Newfoundland Companies; he died in 1878 at the age of ninety-two. My father's family had held land near Tralee in County Kerry since the time of the Cromwellian settlement. My mother was a German, being the daughter of Herr J. F. Ziegler, judge of the Civil and Criminal Court at Curaçao. My father made her acquaintance when he was stationed there with the 60th Rifles after the capture of the place from the Dutch in 1807.

Part of my boyhood was spent in New-foundland, where my father was quartered for some years. My eldest brother, William, died at St. John's at the age of seventeen. I remember that on the day before his death he called his brothers one by one to his bedside and gave us good advice. His words made a very solemn impression on me.

I also had a sister, who died unmarried in Jersey when my father took her there in 1856, in the hope of benefiting her health after his retirement from the army. On the same day as my sister was buried, Richard, another brother, also died. He had intended to be ordained in the Church of England, but abandoning the idea he procured a commission in the Gold Coast Artillery. A younger brother, Frederick, was a lieutenant in the 84th Regiment, and was employed as a captain in the Turkish Contingent during the war with Russia. He afterwards served under General Wheeler during the first part of the Indian Mutiny, but he lost his life in the massacre ordered by Nana Sahib at Cawnpore, into whose hands he and others were betrayed by the rebels. Being taken before the Nana he shot down several of his guards with a revolver, and discharged the last barrel at the Nana himself, but without effect. A few minutes later he was stretched on the ground and cut to pieces. My second brother, Lieut.-Colonel Henry Saunders, who afterwards belonged to the Corps of Gentlemen - at - Arms and was a Military Knight of Windsor, greatly distinguished himself at the re-taking of Cawnpore. The *Times* of that day recorded his gallantry in terms of the highest praise, and mentioned the interesting fact that the place where he behaved so bravely was very

near the spot on which his brother was
murdered.

When I was at St. John's, destructive
fires were of frequent occurrence, as all the
houses and shops were then built of wood.
The country had extensive forests, where
the trees would be cut down in summer, and
brought to the towns in winter on sledges
drawn by dogs. I remember an occasion
on which both sides of a street were in
flames, when my father, who was trying
to extinguish them with the help of his
company, had his face severely scorched
in the process.

The seal and cod fishing contributed
largely to the country's revenue. Quan-
tities of codfish dried in the sun were
exported to Spain and Portugal. The
Newfoundlanders of that day were a tough
race of men, well fitted for the hardships
and the exposure which they had to
endure in their perilous voyages. Their

vessels were bound with iron to resist the pressure of the ice. Sometimes they would bring in between. two and three thousand seals. The lakes and streams in the neighbourhood of St. John's also contained fine trout. It was not uncommon for me and my brothers to bring home eight or ten dozen in one day's fishing with the rod. The summers were hot and the winters excessively cold. Heavy falls of snow and severe frosts afforded ample opportunities for tobogganing and skating, of which I was very fond.

There was a good deal of friction in Newfoundland at this time between High Church and Low Church, as well as between Protestants and Romanists. As an instance of this I may mention an occurrence of which I was a witness. A soldier, a patient in the military hospital, became a convert from Romanism, and requested, in the event of his death, to be buried in the Protestant cemetery. On the day fixed for his funeral the burying-party, which consisted chiefly of soldiers under the command of Captain Grant, on reaching an open space where two roads diverged—the one leading to the Roman Catholic, the other to the Protestant cemetery—was attacked by a mob previously collected at this spot. The coffin was seized and carried off in the direction of the Roman Catholic cemetery. Captain Grant ordered his men to fix bayonets and charge. The crowd took fright, let the coffin fall, and ran away. Captain Grant then marched his men to Fort Townsend and lodged the body there. On arrival Colonel Law, an officer who had fought at Waterloo, ordered all the troops out, supplied them with ammunition, and posted them at the fort gate. Meanwhile a large crowd, with a priest at their head, had assembled. The colonel told the priest that unless he kept his people quiet, and prevented them from further molesting the burying-party, he would give the order to fire. The party then proceeded to the Protestant cemetery in peace. On another occasion the editor of a Protestant newspaper was waylaid at night by masked men, who cut off one of his ears.

Like most young men, I had great difficulty in choosing a definite career. Some of my friends advised me to enter the Church, others to adopt the medical profession. I chose the latter. I had begun to study classics under Mr. Blackman, a Cambridge graduate, and subsequently under Mr. Nugent, a member of the House of Assembly. From both I received the greatest help; but as I was anxious to commence my medical studies in London at once, I spent only a short time over my classical studies; and this I have never ceased to regret up to the present day.

I started for England with my father in

B

1841 for the purpose of entering St. Bartholomew's Hospital. As there was no entrance examination at that time, I was received at once as a registered student. Mr. Wix, the chaplain's son, introduced me to Mr. McWhinnie, the demonstrator of anatomical dissections, who afterwards became my private tutor.

To be suddenly transplanted from my home in Newfoundland to a simple lodging in Devonshire Street, Bloomsbury, and to be a stranger in a crowded city, was an experience not easy to describe. But hard work in the Hospital during the day, and hard work in my rooms till midnight, so fully occupied my thoughts that the time passed pleasantly enough. I lived very simply and took no alcohol. I received particular attention from Edward Stanley, William Laurence, James Paget, and Luther Holden, and, indeed, from all the lecturers in the Hospital.

London at that period was not the same as the London of to-day. The Blue-coat School of Christ's Hospital, which adjoined the Hospital, was then a great centre of young life. Smithfield Market, with its memories of the Protestant martyrs, recorded on a tablet[1] now on the Hospital

---

[1] "Blessed are the dead that die in the Lord."

"*The noble army of martyrs praise Thee.*"

WITHIN A FEW FEET OF THIS SPOT

JOHN ROGERS

JOHN BRADFORT

JOHN PHILPOT

AND OTHER SERVANTS OF GOD

SUFFERED DEATH BY FIRE

FOR THE FAITH OF CHRIST

IN THE YEARS 1555, 1556, 1557.

Near this place is erected a church to the memory of the said martyrs.

walls, used to be crowded with cattle of various kinds. The Holborn Viaduct did not exist. Omnibuses often stuck at the foot of Holborn Hill, so difficult was the ascent for horses. The accidents there supplied many cases for St. Bartholomew's at a time before wood or asphalt paving had been invented.

In the Hospital itself the numerous subjects of study, the changes in the method of pursuing them, the periodical examinations now enforced by the teachers, and the new library, make St. Bartholomew's of to-day a very different place from the one which I entered in 1841. At that time operations had sometimes to be performed at night by candle-light, and it is surprising that in such circumstances the patients should have done well. The dissecting rooms, before the introduction of antiseptic principles associated with the name of Lord Lister, were very disagreeable. Erysipelas,

which used to be so common, has now prac-
cally disappeared by improved ventilation
and other precautions. While I was a
student there, I was fortunate enough to be
awarded the Bentley Prize for surgery, as
well as another for midwifery, and a testi-
monial for anatomy and physiology.

After passing the examination for the
diploma of the Royal College of Surgeons
of England I decided on going to Paris for
further study. I left London by ship for
Boulogne. While waiting at an hotel there
to be shown a room I heard some names
being announced, among them the Duchess
of ———. Having little money to spare,
I thought that such company might be too
much for my slender means, and finding a
diligence ready to start for Paris, I went
on by it at once. I sat in the *coupé* next
the driver, and had a pleasant journey.
The villages through which we passed at
night were then all lighted by oil lamps

suspended on ropes stretched across the streets.

In Paris I took a room in an hotel near the École de Médecine. The expenses of living in those days were much less, and the facilities for study in the French capital were considerably greater, than in England. The theatres of the medical schools were thrown open to the public, and the museums of natural history, with their anatomical and pathological specimens, afforded large opportunities to the learner. The professors were men of high skill and intelligence, and I received much profit from their lectures and clinics, especially from a course on operative surgery by Professor Sappey.

I left Paris in order to enter the Army Medical Department, and after spending some time at the military hospital at Fort Pitt, Chatham, I became an army surgeon in the 47th Regiment. I joined it at

Chester Castle on the 16th December 1845. In the following year the regiment was ordered to Ireland, and while there it was frequently moved about the country, which was in a very disturbed state owing to political agitation. On one occasion, as I recollect, a portion of the regiment was suddenly ordered from Buttevant to Six-mile-Bridge, near Limerick, as disturbances had broken out there between the mob and the military while escorting voters to the polling-booths; and an affray occurred in which some of the soldiers were severely wounded by the stones thrown at them, while two of the rioters were killed. The famine consequent on the failure of the potato crop brought starvation and death in its train, and there was gloom everywhere.

Four years later, when I was stationed at Cork, I was attacked by a serious illness, which prostrated my strength. One day a parcel addressed to me was handed to my servant. On opening it I found a Bible and a note as follows:—"Doctor Saunders' kind acceptance of the accompanying Bible is requested by one who, though a stranger to him personally, yet feels much interest in his soul's welfare, and who, on hearing for the first time his name and illness, besought the Lord not only to raise him up, but also to reveal Himself to him as God and Saviour; for it is the Lord who 'bringeth down to the grave and who bringeth up,' and as He has in mercy spared, may He be pleased to grant the greater thing, even to give Dr. Saunders eternal life; and 'this is life eternal, to know Thee, the only true God, and Jesus Christ whom Thou has sent.'" Inside the cover of the Bible was written: "And one of them, when he saw that he was healed, turned back and with a loud voice glorified God." "I am

the Good Shepherd; the Good Shepherd
giveth his life for the sheep. My sheep
hear my voice, and I know them, and they
follow me; and I give unto them eternal
life; and they shall never perish, neither
shall any man pluck them out of my hand."
I noticed also that several passages were
underlined so as to attract special attention, such as John iii. 14–16; vii. 37, 38;
viii. 12. My first thought was that it was
a sacrilege to mark God's Book in this
way. But later on, and as my strength
began to return, I constantly looked at the
verses marked, and wondered how it was
that I had never before taken any interest
in the Bible, although in my boyhood I
used to attend family prayers and church
and other religious services. Now the
words of Holy Scripture seemed to stand
out in bold relief, as if some hidden power
were at work opening my eyes and heart
to see and believe the truth. Shortly

afterwards I was in great distress of soul. I felt the need of God's help. I found that the world's ways and amusements, in which I had taken such great pleasure, were no longer satisfying. God's Holy Spirit arrested me, convicting me of sin. I felt that I was not fit to die if I were called away. I was convinced that Jesus Christ and He alone was able and willing to deliver me from the judgment to come. Peace and joy came to my soul through faith in Him, and in His finished work. I now began to pray as I had never done before, telling God about the smallest occurrences of my everyday life, especially asking Him for wisdom and judgment in the performance of my military duties, and in the treatment of my hospital patients. I found that I was wonderfully helped in these daily matters. Many of the sick speedily recovered, and the general health of the regiment improved. This greatly encouraged my faith in God. I began for the first time to circulate Gospel tracts, especially those by Ryle, afterwards Bishop of Liverpool, which I considered excellent. I had been much helped by them myself. My trust in God became a great reality, and I was deeply convinced of the truth of the words, "Without Me ye can do nothing."

I was married, on the 15th October 1852, to Isabella, only daughter of Thomas Bailey, J. P., County Fermanagh. Her deep piety and earnestness were a great assistance to me in my spiritual life, and she was ever a most devoted wife. Indeed, it was to her that I really owed my first spiritual awakening; for, as I found afterwards, she was one of two ladies who met to pray for my recovery in that serious illness at the time of my conversion. I first made her acquaintance when I was stationed with my regiment at Buttevant, County Cork, where her father was the resident magistrate. She was then suffering from loss of power in her lower limbs, and as this weakness had continued for about two years she was unable to walk. Her father consulted me about her case, and under my medical care she completely recovered.

I was in the habit of attending soldiers' wives who lived in the neighbourhood, and consequently came into contact with many of the poor. On one occasion I was suddenly and unexpectedly called to a laundress in her confinement. I remained with her for about two hours, when all her troubles were satisfactorily over. As I emerged from the cottage I was startled to find an enormous crowd assembled. The reason of their presence, I was told, was that if the woman had died I should have been murdered.

THE CRIMEAN WAR, 1854–55

ON the declaration of war with Russia by the Allies in 1854, my regiment was ordered to Turkey. I remember that as we embarked at Liverpool on the 10th March the soldiers were heartily cheered by the inhabitants. We on our side were equally demonstrative, little thinking, perhaps, how few of us were likely to return to the shores of Old England. I brought a supply of New Testaments with me from Dublin, and distributed them amongst the soldiers with the earnest prayer that the Lord would bless His Word. We were about to engage in an awful conflict, but the Lord was to be a strong tower and fortress.

When we arrived at Gallipoli, which, like

many Turkish towns, is a miserable place, we found French and English troops encamped in the vicinity. An officer came on board our ship and gave us a deplorable account of the scarcity of provisions there, and the sufferings caused by the cold weather. There was indeed too much truth in the report, current at the time, that there were no proper supplies for the troops at Gallipoli, although some of the authorities would not own to any mismanagement anywhere. At Scutari, too, the troops were accommodated in barracks the reverse of clean, and great confusion prevailed. I had to share a room with three other medical officers, each with a corner to himself.

Among my recollections of Constantinople at the time was a review of British troops held for the Sultan, who appeared in a plain military frock-coat. Attended by a few soldiers he was escorted to the parade-ground by Lord Raglan and the Duke of

Cambridge; and he celebrated the occasion by giving each man a pint of porter. Another was a delightful ride which I took along the Asiatic side of the Bosphorus, enjoying the beautiful scenery and the fragrant air, although the numerous and extensive burial-grounds everywhere produced a melancholy effect. The Grand Bazaar, which I visited, was thronged with Jews engaged in trade, especially in changing money. The Turks themselves I found almost inaccessible to Christian influences.

At Constantinople I often felt that a medical missionary would be the best channel for communicating the glad tidings of the Gospel to these people. There were opportunities of religious instruction then such as has not previously existed. In 1843 Sir Stratford Canning demanded from the Government of the Sultan a pledge, signed by the Sultan himself, that "no person should be persecuted for his religious opinions in Turkey." This demand received the support of the French Government, and after some delay that of the Russian also. It was made because a man had been beheaded for leaving "the true faith," that was Mohammedanism. The custom in such cases was to let the headless body lie on the place of execution for three days, with a placard describing his offence displayed near the spot, and declaring that the man had been taken in the dress of an apostate, and that his offence was apostasy. In this connection I may mention that while there the Secretary of the Auxiliary Bible Society sent me a note, enclosing a resolution which he wished me to second at a meeting to be held at Pera under the presidency of the American Minister. The resolution was to the effect that the circumstances of Turkey at that crisis called for special efforts from Christians of all denominations for the widest possible diffusion of

the Word of God as the best preparative
for whatever events might, in His Provi-
dence, be in store for these lands. While
there, too, the missionaries of the Free
Church of Scotland at Galata gave me a
very affectionate welcome. They appeared
to be doing a good work, including the
keeping of a school, the children of which
were examined in my presence in history,
arithmetic, and the translation of English
into Italian, displaying great efficiency.

From Constantinople we went to Varna,
where the disembarkation was long, tedi-
ous, and badly conducted, so that in the
confusion of tent-pitching, etc., every one
seemed to be the owner of whatever his hand
could reach. No accident that I remember
occurred in spite of many risks run. The
encampment consisted of the 1st and 2nd
divisions of the army, with some French
troops. One night there, while engaged in
prayer, I had a feeling that some one was

near my tent with a loaded musket for some evil purpose. I was so disturbed by it that I got up from my knees and looked out of the tent. All was silent, and scarcely a light was to be seen in the whole camp. Next morning it was reported that one of the sentinels had shot himself.

The surgeon of the regiment having been invalided to England, the colonel, not wishing a fresh one put over my head, recommended me for the vacancy—a step which the authorities approved.

I had the pleasure at Varna of being introduced by his colonel to Captain Hammond of the Rifles. He was a bright and happy Christian, killed afterwards while leading his men at the assault of the Redan. Several years later I met his widow at Venice, where she was engaged in mission work, chiefly among children.

On the 14th September we arrived at Kalamita in the Crimea. We landed unop-

posed on a beautiful sandy beach, marched
off at 5 P.M., and reached our bivouac just
after dark. The rain that night came down
in torrents, and the officers as well as the
men had to lie on the ground in the open
air, wrapped in blankets. The hospital
tent formed an admirable refuge for three
medical officers besides myself and a major
of my regiment who was ill.

We left our encampment on the 19th,
and had a slight brush with the enemy on
the evening of that day, when a few of the
cavalry were wounded. On the following
morning we moved off at 6 A.M., joined the
French, and, with the Turks in the centre
and rear, advanced towards the formidable
position occupied by the Russians at the
river Alma. The great battle there commenced at 1.20 P.M., and was over in about
three hours. The moment our troops came
to close quarters the Russians, by a precon-
certed plan, fired the village of Bourbiouk.

The infantry defiled through the burning
village and immediately extended their
ranks in the open country beyond, then
crossed the river and gained the heights,
which were strongly fortified by one hundred guns and a large force. As long as
the firing lasted the enemy's shot came
among us in all directions, one of them
falling very close to me. On the march
we had been provided with no carts for
the conveyance of the sick and wounded.
Finding that I could not advance with the
rest of the regiment without leaving the
disabled on the field, I seized two arrabas
from the Commissariat, one of which I had
to surrender by Lord Raglan's orders.
When I came to the open country beyond
the river, a ditch was almost filled with my
men. I attended to their wounds with
Dr. Cusack of my regiment, a most skilful
surgeon, and then passed to other parts
of the battlefield, dressing the wounded as

I came upon them. Of all horrible sights that of a battlefield is the worst. The Russians made an excellent retreat. I saw numbers of their dead, and attended many of their wounded; one poor fellow, I remember, whose leg I dressed, was so grateful that he kissed my hand. Our wounded were sent off to the ships to be brought to Scutari.

Our next march was to Balaclava, which fell into our hands without any very great difficulty.

The 2nd division, to which I belonged, was then ordered to occupy the heights of Inkermann. We pitched tents and made ourselves fairly comfortable. But with bad weather, scarcity of provisions, impure water, and insufficient clothing, it was no wonder that there was much hardship and disease. From my position I could hardly see anything of the disastrous charge of the Light Cavalry Brigade under Lord

Cardigan at Balaclava on the 25th October.
Just afterwards I met a staff officer on his
way up from the scene. "The Light
Cavalry Brigade of the British Army does
not exist," he said. Of upwards of 600
who rode down the valley only 200 came
back. The Russians captured a battery
from the Turks. On the next day our
pickets at Inkermann were attacked. The
division under the command of Sir De Lacy
Evans drove back the enemy, who left very
many killed and wounded on the field.
The losses on our side were comparatively
small.

The battle of Inkermann took place on
Sunday the 5th November. It was a
terrible struggle, lasting from daybreak
until 4.30 P.M. During the previous night
the chapel-bells of Sebastopol had been
ringing, as if the Russians had been engaged in their devotions. The night was a
dark and dreary one, and very wet. Very

early in the morning there was much cheering and shouting among the Russians, and evidently great excitement. The confusion of the battle was more than I can attempt to describe. My tent was levelled to the ground by a cannon ball, but providentially I was at one of the hospital tents at the moment. These, too, were riddled with shot and shell, and I had the utmost difficulty in getting my patients beyond the range of fire.

Inkermann was commonly called "the soldiers' battle "—a description borne out by what a young Irishman said to me as I was trying to cheer him up in his wounded condition : " Never mind, sir, we're all our own generals this morning." The battle would never have been fought if proper measures had been taken in time for the defence of our position. Sir De Lacy Evans had in vain remonstrated on the subject. Colonel William O'Grady Haly

of my regiment received four bayonet
wounds, and when on the ground was
attacked by several Russians; had it not
been for the promptness and courage of
Captain Rowlands of the 41st Regiment,
he would have been certainly killed or
captured.   My colonel also had a very
narrow escape at the Alma, where his horse
was shot under him.

The terrible storm of the 14th November,
which caused fearful destruction on sea
and land, affected the whole army, and in
particular the losses outside and inside
Balaclava harbour were very numerous.
The whole of the first part of the cam-
paign, indeed, was conducted under such
trying climatic conditions that they added
materially to its other hardships.   But I
may state here that, in spite of it all, the
patience, courage, and discipline of the
British soldiers could not be surpassed;
and I never heard one of them complain

of the exposure which he had to bear, or the insufficient food and clothing.

Having been promoted to the rank of staff-surgeon, my connection with the 47th Regiment ceased, much to my regret; for I had greatly enjoyed it.

On the 8th December I was ordered to take charge of the sick and wounded proceeding to Scutari. They were transported to the ships by being fastened on to the saddles of cavalry-horses, which were themselves so thin and wretched that they were quite unfit for the purposes of war. About 300 of these poor fellows were put on board with a few officers, the men in a most pitiable state, hungry and thirsty, cold and miserably clad, and often covered with mud, or even vermin. Many of them seemed to be dying, and three of them expired before we left the harbour. It was with the utmost difficulty that I procured the simplest necessities for them,

and the few orderlies whom I had were
ill-trained recruits. As soon as the men
came aboard a large shallow bath was
brought between-decks full of some sort of
pudding, and such of the poor fellows as
could move made for it and began to eat
ravenously; they had had no such treat
since the beginning of the war. The ship
was old and battered, and instead of a
rudder had a portion of a mast attached
to the stern. On my remonstrating with
the port captain, and telling him that such
a ship was hardly seaworthy, he sent a
steamer to accompany us. The make-
shift rudder proved useless, and when we
signalled to the steamer for assistance a
collision took place. The captain of the
convoy then wisely wished us good-bye,
and refused to help us any further. We
then had to do our best to cross the Black
Sea and make for the Bosphorus, where
we anchored. The following morning I

got up early, and was horrified to see a
number of bodies sewn up in blankets and
floating about ; they were of men whose
deaths had occurred during the night. We
did not reach Therapia until the 17th, and
on the 21st two steamers towed us down to
Scutari. In this trying time I was thankful for the able support of Assistant-Sur-
geon Flower (the late Sir William Flower,
K.C.B., Director of the Natural History
Department of the British Museum), who
with myself had to perform many arduous
duties in the absence of an efficient nursing
staff.

I returned to the Crimea on the 3rd
January 1855, and was attached to the
41st Regiment at Inkermann, which was
then without a medical officer ; but owing
to an attack of fever I was sent back again.
On the 12th February I was conveyed in
an open cart to Balaclava, and thence by
steamer to Scutari. Through some mistake

my name was included in the monthly obituary list by Lord Raglan, and my death was announced in the British newspapers. I had to declare that I was still alive.

When I came to Scutari I found that the hospital there had now every appearance of comfort, and was unsurpassed by any other, civil or military. For this improved state of things all the praise was due to the noble and indefatigable efforts of Miss Nightingale, who fortunately had *carte blanche* to do whatever she thought necessary for the comfort and well-being of the sick and wounded. After spending six weeks in hospital I was ordered to England in charge of invalids, reaching Portsmouth on the 5th May. On the 7th June I sailed again for Gibraltar, taking my wife and son with me, as I expected to remain there some time; but on the 11th August I was suddenly ordered to embark for Constanti-

nople. Taking passage in a small steamer,
my wife and son accompanied me. During
the voyage the vessel twice caught fire,
but ultimately we reached our destination
in safety. I had hardly arrived before I
was again ordered to the front, and I had
to leave my wife in a Turkish house at
Scutari. Some of the soldiers of my old
Regiment, the 47th, privately arranged
among themselves to keep guard every
night for her protection—an act of sympathy and kindness not easily forgotten.

I reached the Crimea once more on the
conclusion of the long siege of Sebastopol
which ended in its fall. I recollect riding
down close to the harbour, from which the
Russians had retired towards the north,
and seeing there a large heap of legs and
arms piled up on the beach. While on the
way to look at the Museum a Russian gun
opened fire on me. This was an unpleasant
surprise, as a truce had been called, but

of course I returned with all speed to the British lines.

Finally leaving the seat of war, when I was again in charge of invalids for England, I landed at Portsmouth on the 15th November.

The war cost the Russians nearly 120,000 lives. The final evacuation of the Crimea took place on July 12, 1856.

CAPE COLONY

NEARLY a year later I was ordered to the Cape Colony. My first station after reaching Capetown, on the 16th November 1856, was Port Elizabeth. The night before we arrived there we experienced a fearful storm, through which the old H.M.S. *Penelope* carried us none too securely. Piles of shot got loose and rolled about the flooded decks, adding to our danger. We landed by being carried through the surf on the shoulders of naked Kaffirs.

Almost immediately after my arrival a local baker sent for me to cut off his leg. On visiting the man, I told him that there was no necessity for cutting it off—an

opinion at which he seemed greatly dis-
appointed. Another incident of an en-
tirely different nature, and perhaps more
worth recording, was that a local chaplain
lodged a complaint against me with the
commanding officer that I was in the habit
of interfering with his duties. The ground
of his charge was that I had read the Bible
to a soldier dying of heart disease. The
man was the only patient in hospital at
the time, and he found consolation and
comfort in hearing the Word of God and
joining in prayer. The commanding officer,
hearing my explanation, wrote to the
chaplain in my favour, and the latter
was so annoyed that when he met the
officer shortly afterwards he passed him
by without taking any notice of him. The
officer thereupon said to me, "When I
came here I was as high as the church
steeple, but now I am as low as you
please."

After six months' stay at Port Elizabeth my next move was to Grahamstown, then the headquarters of the troops. Travelling up country in a bullock-waggon with wife and children was quite a new experience and anything but agreeable. Grahamstown was then a prosperous place with a flourishing trade. I remember Bishop Cottrell there, who had not long arrived; it was refreshing and helpful to attend the Bible expositions which he gave in his own house, for he was a man of the old evangelical school, and highly esteemed by the residents of all denominations. I remember, too, being asked by Dr. Campbell, a local practitioner, to visit one of his patients who lived fifteen miles away in the country, and required to be tapped for dropsy. The doctor reminded me of the necessary instrument, but riding off at once through torrential rain I discovered on reaching the house, to my great dismay,

D

that I had forgotten it. The woman's husband immediately said, "I'll saddle up and go for it." "Oh no," I replied. "Show me into a room and leave me alone for a while." I walked up and down the room trying to think how I could manage without it. I then called the husband and asked him whether he had a goose-quill. He said that he had. "Have you a brad-awl?" Yes, he had this as well. I told him to sharpen the brad-awl and bring it to me with the quill. With these materials I made a trocar which answered the purpose admirably, and the patient told me afterwards how very little pain the operation had given her.

While I was at Grahamstown an incident occurred which had both an unpleasant and a gratifying side. It was the custom then and for some time previously for civilians to consult and employ the military medical men stationed in the Colony, regarding them, perhaps, as men of larger experience and fresher knowledge. The military medical men had no formal permission, however, to engage in private practice, but had not been hindered from doing so as long as this did not interfere with their military duties. I had thus acquired a considerable practice when in May 1858 two of the civil medical men made a formal complaint on the subject. The Commander of the Forces, then acting as Lieut.-Governor, took the complaint somewhat too seriously, and strictly limited me to consultation and emergency cases. When his decision became known, a sharp controversy as to its justice and expediency arose in the local newspapers, and there was some public agitation to get it reversed. A memorial to this effect, setting forth the great services which I was believed to have rendered in the town, was signed by upwards of 600 of the inhabitants and duly presented to the Commander of the Forces. After considering it he issued a general order authorising all the military medical officers at that station to render their professional assistance of any kind when by so doing their military duties did not suffer. As usually happens on a man's being unsuccessfully attacked, my practice and general reputation were only increased by the incident.

My next station was Middle Drift, close to the river Keskama. From this post I had several other military posts to visit, which involved my being constantly on horseback. One of my first calls was to see a soldier who had been murdered by Kaffirs. I had to cross the river in the middle of the night—a very rapid river at the time—with a mounted orderly at each side of me; and had it not been for their protection I should probably have been swept away.

Having been appointed district surgeon by the Colonial Government, my duties extended to the Kaffir population. An epidemic of small-pox broke out in a native village. As soon as I arrived on the scene I observed some Kaffirs dragging a corpse which they had placed on a bush with long ropes attached, in order to bury it far away; they were going to bury one of the victims of the disease. Three other cases were isolated in a hut, with watchers to prevent them escaping. Food was left for them about two hundred yards from the hut, if they were able to walk for it. I rode up to the village, and as I approached men and women ran into their huts to avoid contagion. I captured a little child, and after vaccinating it, rode off again. Six days afterwards I again visited the village, and the natives, finding that the child which I had vaccinated did not take small-pox, immediately offered to be vaccinated themselves. No more cases occurred, while in the villages beyond my jurisdiction hundreds suffered and a great many died.

It is worth recording that a splendid work among the natives was then being carried on at the Lovedale Seminary and Mission by the Free Church of Scotland, where I had the pleasure of meeting Tio Soga, a very intelligent Kaffir missionary who had married a Scotch lady. The Lovedale Institution had the great advantage of being industrial as well as religious. My intercourse with the missionaries was very agreeable.

After spending five years at the Cape I embarked for England with my wife and four children at Port Elizabeth on the 22nd August 1861. Our voyage on board the sailing ship *William* lasted seventy-six days. Touching at St. Helena, my wife and I, with the captain, visited the grave where

Napoleon's remains had lain for upwards
of twenty years before being removed to
Paris, and also his residence at Longwood.
The ship was leaky, and gave the pumps
plenty to do. Our chronometers were out
of order, and one night after entering the
English Channel the captain discovered by
soundings that we were not far off the
French coast; and the wind being contrary,
he was most anxious. The wind continuing
to blow us towards the coast, my wife and
I prayed that God would be pleased to save
us from disaster; and a short time afterwards the wind changed to a sou'-west gale,
which so favoured us that the ship went
up Channel at good speed under little
canvas. In due course we reached the
English shore in safety and with thankful
hearts.

Shortly after my arrival I was appointed
to the medical charge of the 14th depôt
battalion at Belfast. Two years later I

remember Mr. Grattan Guinness preaching there with great power at some most remarkable meetings in that city. Numbers of his hearers confessed to having received blessing.

CHINA AND JAPAN

ON the 27th September 1864 I was
appointed surgeon to the second battalion of the 9th Regiment. Leaving my
wife and family at home, I joined at
Gibraltar. This was my third visit to
the famous Rock, a pleasant and healthy
station. Learning that the destination of
the regiment was shortly to be Hong-
Kong, and knowing how severely previous
regiments, especially the 59th, had suffered there from sickness, I communi-
cated with experienced medical officers on
the subject of the climate and the pre-
valent diseases. I received the most
distressing accounts, and was assured
that many of my men would certainly

be left in the " Happy Valley " (*i.e.* the cemetery).

We sailed from Gibraltar on the 3rd of November in H.M.S. *Tamar*, commanded by Captain Stirling, R.N., and reached Hong-Kong on the 7th February 1865. We stayed for a short time on our way out at the Cape and Singapore, and anchored for one night off Batavia (Java), having a pleasant voyage throughout.

Not long after our arrival at Hong-Kong the native Indian troops were ordered back to their country, English regiments taking their place. The exchange, I believe, was made with a view to economy, but it only resulted in increased expenditure, and, what was worse, lamentable mortality. The guard and other duties devolving on the new arrivals were excessive by day and night, while the barrack accommodation and the provision

for the sick were very insufficient. More-
over, the summer season turned out a
very hot and unhealthy one, and cholera,
dysentery, and epidemic fever prevailed
among the soldiers as well as the civil
population. The work which then fell to
me to do was of the most arduous and
responsible character, as I was acting
principal medical officer of the station.
I am happy to say that I was enabled to
perform it to the complete satisfaction of
the authorities, and was fortunate enough
to have my name brought to the favour-
able notice of the War Office in despatches.
Indeed, the recognition which my services
received was particularly gratifying; for,
as I may perhaps be allowed to mention,
attention was drawn to them in the House
of Commons by Colonel North, M.P. for
North Oxfordshire, and again by Colonel
Sankey of the 9th Regiment, in the
evidence which he gave before a Select

Committee of the House on the mortality of the troops in China (July 1866).

The duties of the military medical officers were so heavy that I had to apply to the senior naval officer for the services of two of the ships' surgeons, which he readily granted. In the course of a few months the health of the 11th Regiment became so bad that it was struck off duty for a time; and by my representations the authorities decided to charter a vessel and send as many as possible of the disabled to England. It was joyful news when these men received orders "to prepare for home." The vessel hired was the *Gresham*, a fine ship fitted up for emigrants at Hong-Kong, and available at the time; but a number of the invalids died at sea between that port and the Cape.

The merchants and residents of Hong-Kong have always been noted for their

generous hospitality, and the regiment
came in for a good share of it, so that
our stay there was made as agreeable as
could be. I once paid a week's visit to
Canton by a passenger steamer with a
great many Chinese coolies on board, who
were not allowed on the upper deck for
fear of mutiny. The captain when at
dinner kept a brace of loaded revolvers by
him in case any sudden outbreak should
compel him to use them. Such an outbreak
was nothing uncommon in Chinese waters.
The coolies on land would sometimes pass
the sentries unobserved at night, enter
the officers' rooms at the Murray Barracks,
and steal jewellery or other valuables.

I remember that one evening at Hong-
Kong, after mess, the conversation turned
on the performances given by the officers
of the regiment in a theatre which they
had built there for their amusement and
that of their friends. The colonel jokingly

said to me, "We shall see you, Saunders, one of these days, on the stage." "I shouldn't mind, colonel," I replied, "for in my former regiment I used to take part in such performances." The colonel was surprised. "That's capital; what day will you come?" he asked. "Any day you like, colonel; Monday, Tuesday, Wednesday, or even Sunday; Sunday would suit me very well, and for scenery I shall only want the curtain." He answered most kindly, "Let us say Sunday, then, and I shall be there." Thus it came about that Sunday evening services for preaching the Gospel were regularly held until the regiment was ordered to Japan. The attendance was fairly good, and on our way to Yokohama on board the troopship the colonel begged me to continue them, which the naval officer in command permitted me to do. A weekly Bible-class was also held in my quarters in Murray

Barracks for both naval and military officers. A captain of my regiment entered the room for the first time just as we had assembled one day. He sat down and joined in our reading. We had only read a few verses when he exclaimed, "Oh, how wonderful! I never saw that before." I saw him again long afterwards, in 1902, at Hampstead, when he was in a dying state but very happy. Although his sufferings were very great, his patience under them was extraordinary. He was perfectly content to leave this world and be with Jesus; and his last words to me were, "This world is nothing but vanity."

We arrived at Yokohama in May 1866. I soon became acquainted with Dr. Hepburn, an American missionary, who held a Bible-class for the Japanese at which many attended. It was most interesting and helpful to see how anxious they were to understand the Scriptures. The doctor

was a splendid missionary, and my acquaintance with him led me to form a
high opinion of American missionaries in
general, as men of remarkable zeal, ability,
and perseverance.

A few days after my arrival a Japanese
lady who was ill requested me to visit her.
I found her suffering from fever. On her
recovery she made a parasol, and presented
it to me, as a token of her gratitude.

Yokohama lies at the foot of the volcanic
mountain Fujiyama, which, 12,370 feet high,
stands out very grandly over the city. We
experienced frequent shocks of earthquake
there. I remember being nearly thrown
out of my bed one night, and as I thought
that the house was coming down I made
for the door; but by the time I reached
it the shock was over. In walking about
one often felt the ground moving. While
I was there, three daimios, two-sworded
men, requested that I would instruct them

in medicine. They visited the military hospital every morning, and it was remarkable how intelligent and observant they were in taking notes. Each had a book divided into columns, with such headings as " Disease, Treatment, Diet, Medicine," and in the last column any special observations which I made on each case at the bed-side. They would then repair to the dispensary to examine the medicines prescribed, noting the colour and weight of the various drugs and the smell of the tinctures, &c. I told them that it was absolutely necessary, in order to make any solid progress in medical knowledge, to study anatomy by dissection. On hearing this they politely bowed, and informed me that their Government would not allow it. This was long before the Revolution, by which things were greatly changed, and the Japanese, obtaining their liberty, became a first-class power. My experience

E

is that, where no religious liberty prevails and priests bear rule, there is always much superstition.

In August 1866 I was invalided from Japan, and returned home to my wife and family, then living in Dublin. On the voyage I made a brief stay at Shanghai, and had the opportunity of visiting a leper-house—one of the most painful sights I ever witnessed.

ENGLAND

SOON after my return to England I was
offered the post of sanitary officer to the
Abyssinian Expedition, but in view of my
health and other circumstances I decided
to decline it. A little later, and after a
period of sick-leave, I was appointed, in
June 1867, to the staff of the Bristol
recruiting district, where I resided for
some time at No. 7 Royal York Crescent,
Clifton. Many of the recruits, who came
from various places, were careless and
indifferent; some had run away from their
homes, and others had left their employ-
ments to enter the army. I commenced
to hold Bible and prayer-meetings for
them, which I was compelled by order to

discontinue. Then I began to distribute Testaments to those who could read; at that time very few could do so. Although my mouth was stopped, the Word of God was not. In the different stations where my lot has been cast at home or abroad, at sea or on land, I was enabled by God's grace to get soldiers and others together for prayer and the reading of the Scriptures.

At Bristol it was my happy privilege to become personally acquainted with Mr. George Müller during the last three years of my military service. My attention was aroused by the great stress which Mr. Müller laid on the Word of God, and the earnestness with which he urged his hearers to believe and act on what God had said, and the importance of waiting on God to be taught by the Holy Spirit. This struck me as a prominent feature of his work and ministry. The Orphanage under his management was a monument of God's mercy.

On the 14th February 1871, I retired from the army after a period of twenty-five years' service, being raised to the honorary rank of Deputy-Inspector-General of Hospitals, and having previously had the Companionship of the Bath conferred on me. Never can I forget the happy time that I spent in the old 47th Regiment, and also in the second battalion of the 9th. The brotherly feeling existing among the officers, and the *esprit de corps* of both regiments, could not be surpassed.

As to my future, I was undecided whether to undertake private practice or to enter some specially Christian work. I knew from experience that medical missions offered a wide and valuable field for doing good, particularly among the poor. While I was hesitating, my decision was taken on the receipt of a letter asking whether I would carry on the medical mission at Liverpool, as the dispensary was closed through the illness of the superintendent, Dr. Owles. I consented to help in the work for three months from the 15th April 1871; and I arrived in Liverpool on that day, receiving a warm welcome from the doctor and his wife. The work was enormous, for men, women, and children attended the mission in crowds, giving the doctors, nurses, and lady helpers plenty to do. The chief object was to heal the sick and preach the Gospel; and the best results were to be found in personal dealing with the people, as many had to be visited who were too ill to leave their rooms. Dr. and Mrs. Owles were of one mind with my wife and myself in the method of work; and some of the worst characters which we encountered underwent a complete change of life through the success which God was pleased to give to our efforts.

I remember about this time paying a short visit to Edinburgh, where I had the good fortune to meet Dr. Burns Thomson, the pioneer of medical missions. He was a man overflowing with enthusiasm about them, and he gave me some valuable counsel on their management. Paying a short visit to the Royal Infirmary, there I became acquainted with the present Lord Lister, then a professor seeing his patients in the wards. I was attracted by his courteous and friendly manner, and the eager way in which he explained to me the treatment of surgical operations on antiseptic principles. I happened to mention a plan which I had adopted on board a ship crowded with sick and wounded from the Crimea, using a diluted form of chlorate of sodium for washing the bodies and dressing the wounds of the soldiers between-decks, where the air was most offensive; under this treatment, I told him, the wounds very soon became healthy. Lister's face lit up with intense delight. "That's it!" he exclaimed, "that's it!"

During a stay in Cumberland, when I was feeling the need of relaxation for mind and body, I got a letter asking whether I would undertake the work of a medical mission just established in London. By a subsequent post a similar offer was made to me on behalf of Bristol, and a third to join the one at Liverpool permanently. The invitation from London coming first, I resolved to accept it, and shortly afterwards I settled at 10 (later 28) Colville Terrace, W.

The foundation of THE LONDON MEDICAL MISSION came about as follows :— In October 1869, Dr. Burns Thomson had delivered an address at Queen's Square House, London, which resulted in a committee being formed to set up a medical mission there such as he advocated. Shortly afterwards Mr. Hugh Matheson secured the lease of No 13 Endell Street, St. Giles, W.C., for this purpose. It was not, however, till early in 1871 that the work was begun, when Dr. Waring, Dr. MacAlden, and Dr. Ward, each volunteered to attend one day a week, and Dr. Heath Strange [1] undertook the duties of secretary. The arrangement made no provision for patients unable to leave their homes, since physicians in private practice could not spare the time to visit them; and in order to supply this need it became essential for some one to be appointed able to devote himself to the work. A committee consisting, among others, of Messrs. W. D.

[1] Died on February 28, 1907.

Anderson, James E. Mathieson, Hugh Matheson, Joseph Weatherly, John Grant, and Dr. A. C. Stewart was constituted, and in May 1871 issued a circular, from which I may reproduce the following passages :—

"Is there any Scriptural agency for calling public attention to this subject? Has the Master announced, and have His followers acted on the principle, that the body is worthy of *His* care who took flesh and dwelt among us? Very strikingly the commission was given to the twelve: He sent them to 'preach the kingdom of God and to heal the sick'; and more strikingly to the seventy missionaries who went forth, two and two, before His face: 'Heal the sick, and say unto them that the kingdom of God is come nigh unto you.'

"This addition to existing agencies needs no apology; for the miserable condition of the poor—morally, physically, and spiritually—is a loud call to all Christians for hearty co-operation in the promotion of a work so peculiarly fitted to meet the urgent requirements of the dark places of our great cities; and one on which God has already been graciously pleased to bestow a rich blessing, wherever it has been undertaken in the spirit of faith and love, whether at home or abroad. Practical sympathy with human suffering is unquestionably the key to unlock the entrance to many a heart otherwise closed to the truth."

The mission attracted a good deal of attention in the public press. Several newspapers published accounts of the St. Giles' district. The *British Messenger* stated that such a mission had ample scope there for all appliances for the good of soul and body, as the district was widely known, by name at least, as one of the worst, socially, morally, and spiritually, in London.

The *Daily Telegraph* in 1873 described St. Giles' as the headquarters of depravity and squalor, like a legacy from the barbarous past; and went on to say that no less than a hundred and seventy of the notorious St. Giles' cellars were still in use as human habitations, and that, after the manner of rats and other burrowing animals, as many families, consisting of mother, father, and a more or less numerous swarm of big and little children, passed their lives in those dismal holes under the houses, eating, drinking, and sleeping all in the damp and dirt and dark. It was also reported that there were 3000 families there living each in one room, and that, while the average mortality in all London was 21.5 per thousand, among those families the mortality was between 40 and 50 per thousand. The death-rate among infants and young children was very great, owing to unsuitable food, impure air, insufficient clothing, and want of care on the part of parents.

A body of trustees took over the premises, and a committee of twenty-six influential Christian men appointed me as the first superintendent of this mission. I entered on the work in October 1871, fully aware of its responsible character, but casting myself upon God and committing my labours into His hands. Friends were raised up to help and encourage me; and among these I must specially mention Mr. J. E. Mathieson, whose whole heart was in such work, and whose long-continued kindness and sympathy I can never forget. This missionary effort was necessarily undenominational, and it soon commended itself to a great many people both at home and abroad. I had had practical experience of the value of such effort at Birr in Ireland,

and in Liverpool, as well as among the
Kaffirs in Africa, the Chinese in Hong-
Kong, and the Japanese in Yokohama.

In the following two years, however, the
demands of the work rapidly increased, and
all those who took part in it found their
strength severely taxed in attending to the
various calls upon them. Difficulties also
arose in regard to funds, as I found it
impossible to perform my medical duties
and at the same time engage in the labour
of collecting contributions, which the committee hoped that I should be able to
undertake. An arrangement was eventually
reached by which the committee resigned,
leaving me as sole director under the
trustees, who continued their good offices.
From this time onwards the financial ques-
tion was largely solved by the generosity
of numerous donors and subscribers, stimu-
lated, doubtless, by the appearance of annual

reports and occasional papers describing the success of the mission.

Contributions in kind were also made. The first gift of clothing for the sick was brought by Miss Annie Butler, who up to the previous day had been ignorant of the mission's existence. Passing through Endell Street she was surprised and delighted to see the words *London Medical Mission* on the outside of the house. Her first thought was, "What can I do for it?" She paid us a visit, and joined our prayer-meeting, at that moment being held, requesting prayer for a similar work being started in Birmingham—a city which now has a very flourishing mission of its own. The Hon. J. E. Gordon, too, also had his attention drawn to the work by the fact that he was engaged in a house-to-house visitation in connection with the evangelistic services then being held by

Messrs. Moody and Sankey; and shortly afterwards, having been presented with a sum of money, he forwarded it to us. He helped in our Sunday-school and in a movement for establishing a Holiday House in connection with the mission. Even after he became a Member of Parliament his interest in the work continued.

When the patients were assembled in the waiting-room each morning it was our custom to hold a Gospel service lasting about fifteen minutes, and we hope that good resulted from it. The hand of sickness and often of death was upon many of those present, and they had to be addressed with all tenderness and compassion. During the first six months no less than 2,357 cases came for medical treatment. They were of varied callings—cabmen, costermongers, fruit and flower sellers, tramps and drunkards, poor women with babies in their arms, &c.; many of them in direst need and utterly destitute. Various nationalities, including a large number of Jews, were to be found among them. The patients increased so rapidly that the two adjoining houses in Short's Gardens had to be purchased and adapted for the purpose of the work. I had also to secure the assistance of a second doctor, besides two nurses; and lady helpers also gave their services.

One or two particularly pathetic cases I may here recall. I remember five little children crying, "Mother is dead and we are left alone," as they rushed out of the dark passage of a house in Little Wild Street one Sunday evening. Heavy rain was falling, and the sight of them was pitiable and distressing. They drew up around me as I stopped to inquire what was the matter. The eldest replied, "Mother is in

the coffin, father is out, and we are alone."
I found that the mother had died of consumption, leaving a baby eight months old,
thus making six children in all. Another
case was that of a young man in the last
stage of the same disease, and living in
a gloomy cellar in New Compton Street.
His wife, with a baby in her arms, stood by
his bedside, and the cellar showed extreme
poverty. She explained that he had been
employed in a shop near Seven Dials, and
received eighteen shillings a week, but
seven months previously had been obliged
to give up his work, as he could do it no
longer. Compelled to leave his room in
Neal Street, he had been allowed to occupy
the cellar free of charge through the kindness of a friend. He seemed cheered and
comforted as I spoke to him of Jesus, the
Friend who was able to save all who came
to Him. The mission stores provided him

with more bedclothes, as well as things for his wife and child, besides food and coals; so that he was well cared for to the day of his death. A third case was that of a girl who had been placed in an Irish convent by her step-father and then brought by her mother to live in St. Giles'! Here the step-father shut her out of the house by day and made her sleep on the stairs by night. The girl fell into consumption, and it was a great privilege to minister to her necessities. I could mention many other cases of a similar kind, but these will suffice to show with what distress and destitution we had to deal. It is heart-rending to think what numbers there are in our great cities still on the verge of starvation—men, women and children struggling for bare existence within a stone's-throw of the greatest affluence and luxury. It is a fearful reproach to our social system, and to the various religious sects warring with one another instead of co-operating in the effort to introduce a better state of things.

The Word of God and prayer always held its place in the work of the mission. On visiting the patients in their homes I usually read out of their own Bibles, where they had them, rather than out of mine; because, being as a rule unacquainted with the Scriptures, they could hardly believe that another copy was the same as theirs; and they would thus discover that they had all along possessed a treasure without being aware of it. My wife held a Bible-class, at which every one was expected to take a share in the reading. I re-collect one poor woman declaring that she had been greatly struck by the words "All flesh is grass," as it came to her turn, and recalling the fact when one of the nurses brought her some flowers one day with the same words attached on a card. Before she died she made her husband promise to attend the class; but after coming twice he, too, died a few weeks later, having, as we hoped, received the same blessing as his wife.

In 1876 a Convalescent Home for women was opened at Folkestone, intended for patients recovering from illness, and for others who could pay a portion of their expenses. In a short time the freehold of the house selected became the property of the mission through the generosity of friends, one of whom gave £500 on the strict condition that his name was never to be mentioned. A solicitor, too, did the business of the conveyance free of charge. The inaugural meeting was attended by many who came to pray for blessing on this extension of our work, and its results were very encouraging. Under the later management of Miss Kate Brown it has been productive of much good to its inmates, both physically and spiritually.

It was the Hon. J. E. Gordon who first drew our attention to the advantage which we might derive from having a Holiday House in connection with the mission, to be devoted to giving change of air and bright surroundings to poor children in need of those blessings. Similar houses, he told us, had been established in Denmark, Germany and Switzerland. We accordingly hired a house in the little village of Essendon in Hertfordshire, and on the 4th May 1878 the first party arrived. A lady in the immediate vicinity showed a warm interest in the undertaking, not only by contributing to the expenses of it, but also by entertaining the children at tea in her own grounds. The institution has been continued ever since, though in other localities, and with equally beneficial results. One of my daughters assisted in the conduct of the House. She, having most successfully managed a large singing-class and services for the boys and girls at the mission, was regarded as their friend. She also started a little savings' bank to encourage them to save their pennies and thus promote habits of thrift. Sometimes, too, clothing and boots were supplied them as required.

In connection with the work of the mission I may mention that I was greatly interested in the formation of a Medical Prayer Union. Something of the same kind had been started in 1849 by Dr. Habershon for members of the medical profession, and in 1853 he and Dr. Golding Bird had formed the "Christian Medical Association" both for doctors and students. This, however, ceased to exist about the year 1871. In the following year an attempt to found another association with the object of promoting the spiritual welfare of medical students was made by Mr. Hyde, a student of King's College, London, and myself; but nothing effectual was accomplished until 1874, when I arranged with Dr. Fairlie Clarke, of Charing Cross Hospital, to hold a conference at Endell Street with such medical men and students as were likely to be interested in the matter. Of this conference the Medical Prayer Union was the result; its purpose was to establish Bible and prayer-meetings at the various metropolitan medical schools, to be arranged and conducted by the students themselves. Several of the teachers lent their assistance, and encouraged the movement with much zcal.

In November of the same year we held
our first annual meeting at Freemasons'
Hall under the presidency of Dr. Habershon, and at this and subsequent annual
meetings testimony was borne to the utility
of our aims by Mr. Le Gros Clark, F.R.S.,
Dr. A. P. Stewart, Dr. Fairlie Clarke, and
others. I recollect a striking address delivered on one of these occasions by the
late Sir Arthur Blackwood. " There is,"
he said, " perhaps no higher or nobler
profession in this world than that of medical men. But, if you have been entrusted
with the power to go amongst your fellow-
creatures to heal and bind up their wounds
in a material sense, none the less, I repeat
it, by the fact of your union with your
Lord and Master, are you entrusted by a
higher Authority than any on earth can
give with the glorious privilege of pro-
claiming healing to the broken-hearted

and the recovering of sight to the spiritually blind. It is in your power to bear
the sweet message of life to many whom
none else in this world, it may be, can
reach. You can reach them in hours of
distress, sorrow, pain and suffering. The
glorious Gospel of the blessed God is
committed to your trust." The steady
growth of the Union was remarkable, for
by 1880 nine of the eleven medical schools
held meetings weekly for Bible study and
prayer, with a total membership of 250.
Two of the members went as medical
missionaries abroad, namely, Dr. Schofield
to China and Dr. Lord to India.

Meanwhile another union with similar
aims had been formed by Dr. Fairlie Clarke
and myself in the Medical Missionary
Association, for the purpose of assisting
such Christian work at home and abroad
as might lie within the sphere of medical

agencies. Its special object was to collect and diffuse information regarding the need for medical missions everywhere. A journal was soon published entitled *Medical Missions at Home and Abroad;* it was first edited by Dr. Fairlie Clarke, and afterwards by Dr. James Maxwell, formerly a medical missionary in Formosa, and then director of a medical students' training - home at Highbury.

At length, in 1882, I felt that, with every prospect of the mission being able to continue its good work and make still further progress, the time had arrived when I might seek the rest and refreshment of which I stood in need. It was painful to me to have to leave the many sufferers who required assistance in their distress, and I was glad to be able to look forward to a change of scene, knowing that others would gladly and efficiently carry on the work which I was relinquishing. During the last twenty-five years I have led what some might describe as a retired life, although it has not been without activity in the Medical Mission cause. Of late I have had my share of personal sorrow in the death of my beloved wife, who passed away in perfect peace at Crowborough, Sussex, on the 15th September 1903, in the 82nd year of her age; of my eldest son, who died in New Zealand; and of one of my grandsons, a midshipman, who died off Cyprus—all of them within twelve months of one another. But on looking back over the varied scenes and experiences of my career, I feel that I have much cause for thankfulness. Life has been full of interest to me, and has given me a great deal to enjoy in the society of my many friends and companions. Above all, and beyond any earthly pleasure or satisfaction, has been the love of God in my heart—to me an unworthy sinner saved by grace. The interests, the pleasures, the duties of life pass away : but the salvation which Christ gives, He gives for ever.

Reader, will you refer once again to the letter which was sent me when I was a young man (see page 24), and take it as a message to yourself ?

THE END

.

Printed by BALLANTYNE, HANSON & Co.
Edinburgh & London